A Loo[k at]
Pets

Written by Christine Butterworth

Harcourt
Supplemental Publishers

Rigby • Steck-Vaughn

www.steck-vaughn.com

Contents

Kinds of Pets 3

Finding a Pet 6

Taking Care of a Pet 10

The Right Pet for You 22

Index 24

Some people keep snakes
and lizards as pets.

Kinds of Pets

Lots of people keep dogs and cats as pets. But some people choose different pets. They choose animals like snakes and lizards.

Cats and dogs make good family pets. They like to be around people. Snakes and lizards can be good pets, too. Some of them can live for a long time. Some snakes live to be 40 years old!

In this book, you can learn about cats, dogs, snakes, and lizards. Just turn to the next chapter to find out more!

Dogs make good pets because they like to be with people.

Finding a Pet

You can get a cat or dog at a pet store. You can get one at an animal shelter, too. Sometimes you can get a cat or dog from a family. The family just wants a good home for the cat or dog.

A dog from an animal shelter needs a good home.

You can get a snake or lizard from a pet store. Snakes and lizards need special care. You need to talk to a vet before you get one. The vet can tell you how to care for a snake or lizard.

A vet can tell you how to care for a snake or lizard.

Taking Care of a Pet

Your dog or cat may want to sleep next to you. But your pet needs its own place to sleep. A dog needs a bed to lie on. A cat needs its own place to sleep, too.

A dog needs its own bed.

Snakes and lizards can't keep themselves warm. Your snake or lizard has to live in a warm tank. The tank needs to be big. Why? Your snake or lizard may be small when you get it. But it can grow to be as big as you!

Snakes and lizards need lots of room to grow.

You can get dog food or cat food in a pet store. Cats and dogs need to eat just one or two times a day. They need to eat dry food. Dry food is good for their teeth. Cats and dogs also need clean water to drink every day.

Dry food keeps cats' teeth clean.

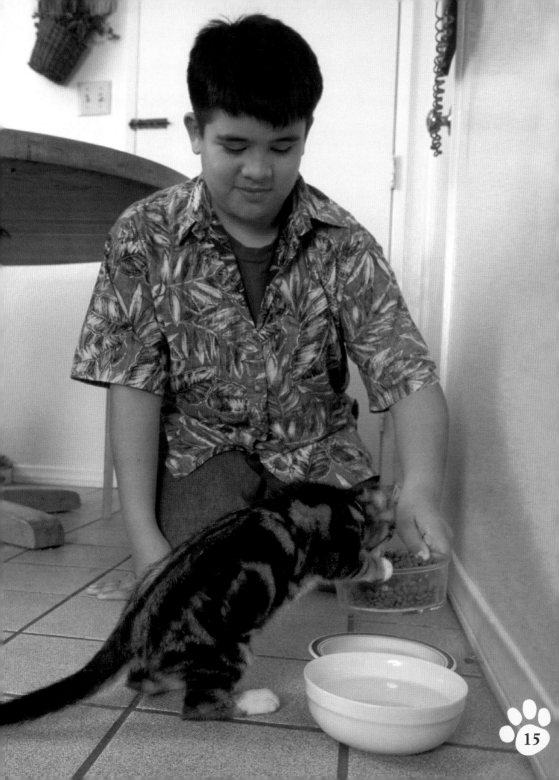

Some lizards eat bugs or other small animals every day. Some snakes just eat small animals once a week. You can get bugs and other small animals from a pet store. Snakes and lizards also need clean water to drink every day.

Many lizards eat baby insects.

You need to keep your cat or dog healthy. Cats and dogs need to walk, run, and play. A dog needs a walk every day.

You need to keep your cat or dog clean, too. Cats wash themselves, but dogs don't. You need to wash your dog.

A dog needs a bath when it's dirty.

You need to keep your snake or lizard healthy, too. You need to keep its tank clean. You can get sand and plants for the tank. Lizards like a rock to lie on. They like a place to hide, too.

Lizards like plants to climb.

The Right Pet for You

A vet can tell you more about how to take care of a pet. You can talk to people who have the same kind of pet, too.

	Cats and Dogs
Where to Get a Pet	• At a pet store • At an animal shelter • From a family
What a Pet Needs	• A good home • A bed to sleep in • Running • Playing • Dry food to eat • Clean water to drink
The Right Pet for You	• Make good family pets • Like to be around people

Before you get a pet, find out a lot about it. Books like this one can help you get the right pet for you.

Snakes and Lizards
• At a pet store
• A big, warm tank to live in • A rock to lie on • Bugs or other small animals to eat • Clean water to drink
• Live for a long time

Index

Animal shelter   6

Cat   3, 4, 6, 10, 14, 18

Dog   3, 4, 6, 10, 14, 18

Food   14

Lizard   3, 4, 8, 12, 16, 20

Pet store   6, 8, 14, 16

Snake   3, 4, 8, 12, 16, 20

Vet   8, 22

Water   14, 16